The
PIMP
Playbook

The Psychology Of Pimpology

VOLUME #1

Written & Created By
Delano B. Gurley

"It's not matrimony, it's macaroni."

-Pimpin Ken

The information provided herein is stated to be truthful and consistent, in that any liability, in terms of inattention or otherwise, by any usage or abuse of any policies, processes, or directions contained within is the solitary and utter responsibility of the recipient reader.

Under no circumstances will any legal responsibility or blame be held against the publisher for any reparation, damages, or monetary loss due to the information herein, either directly or indirectly.

Respective authors own all copyrights not held by the publisher. The information herein is offered for informational purposes solely, and is universal as so. The presentation of the information is without contract or any type of guarantee assurance.

The trademarks that are used are without any consent, and the publication of the trademark is without permission or backing by the trademark owner. All trademarks and brands within this book are for clarifying purposes only and are the owned by the owners themselves, not affiliated with this document.

All Wisdom Works If You Work It!

The Definition Of Pimpology

Pimpology refers to the study of Pimping and the psychology behind it. Pimpology teaches principles that show you how to control and manipulate others, by understanding the principles of human psychology.

Pimpology is effective because most people have no knowledge of brain psychology. This makes their minds extremely vulnerable to those who understand the basic principles. Pimpology is the study of these basic principles.

These principles make up the techniques and mindsets learned in this wisdom. And these principles named Pimpology empower an individual to manipulate the minds of others and move them into action.

This is what Pimpology is and what Pimpology does for the individual who becomes a Master. The one who studies Pimpology will be rewarded greatly with the knowledge and self and others, therefore learning the habits of the human mind as a result of his own mind.

"When I speak of love,

it's pimping I'm speaking of."

-Pimpin' Ken

Table Of Pimping

The Player, The Pimp & The Mack

<u>A Player</u> - He wants **Sexual Gratification**

• He wants to sleep with as many women as possible

• He uses game to get women in bed

<u>A Mack</u> - He wants **Power**

• He wants power because it brings sex and money

• He uses all his skills to get people to submit to him

<u>A Pimp</u> - He only wants the **Money**

• Not interested as much in the pussy

• He uses his mind to guide his women

The Game Is To Be Sold, And Not Told

"Never give game for free, without a fee!"

• You have to be selected to get the game, or through a form of payment

• Whenever you give someone something for free it's never appreciated

• We appreciate what we pay for because we traded something of value for it

• You'll find the people that you made pay for it, are the ones that actually receive change from it

Wise Words To A Pimp

• All of us are just looking for a love that we've never had

• When you put drugs in your brain, you lose your game

• Play this game fair, and this game will play fair with you

• The game of life knows exactly what you put in, and that's the only thing you're going to get back

• Knowledge of the pimp game will benefit your life greatly

• When you spit your game to others, they gotta accept it. They can't help but to. That's when you know that you've mastered the game

• What makes a life a legacy is when people not only tell stories about you, but also the stories you told

Pimp......

"Play this game fair, and this game will play fair with you."

-Pimpin Ken

What's A Pimp?

A Pimp is an energetically masculine man. This forces her to be in her feminine energy if she wants to interact peacefully with him. A feminine woman wants to feel protected by a masculine man, instead of feeling masculine and having to protect her feminine man.

You have to be the reason why she wants to become feminine. This is what she wants to feel like with a man she respects. Someone will always bow down their energy to the other. No two masculine energies can exist at the same time and she has to submit or leave with the pimp.

Someone will have to be masculine or feminine energy even when two men interact. Pimps understand game! Having game simply just means you have a strategy which is the result of a combined knowledge of self and wisdom of the world.

*The Proper Knowledge + Life Wisdom = **Game***

Pimps understand the different types of games people play. Everyone has a motivation and a strategy in the game of life but not everyone's game is the same. The key is that Pimps know the mind games people play and can quickly notice when they're being used on him or others.

For example, most men use a lot of short term strategies with women just for sex. While women use primarily long term strategies with men to get the security of a relationship for themselves. Pimps use many of the same long term strategies that women use on men.

Why: Because she can't see when her own game is being used on her until it's too late because she's emotionally hooked. Once she's in "love" with you, her judgement and decision making will always be foggy with her "love" for you. Now she'll do what you want her to do for you.

Pimps also understand that women are built to take a man's energy. Her strategy is to get what you value most for her own gain. Your energy comes in the forms of your money, your resources and your attention.

A woman has her wants and needs as her priority but so does a Pimp. Just like she wants a man's energy, the pimp wants to use her energy also, not just get in her pants. Unlike most men who prioritize the pussy above everything else.

Because a pimp plays her own game against her he sets himself apart from the short term strategy of getting pussy that most men use. So ultimately he gets access to the pussy but he also gets to access her energy, her time and her money.

He gets full access into her energy because a pimp makes her earn what she gets. This pushes her to want his energy so she submits to him. He doesn't try to wine and dine her just to get pussy like most men. He wants her to value what he gives so he makes her work for it.

This is the opposite of how most men play the game by thinking that he can earn her respect, keep access to her pussy and long term admiration if he gives her whatever she wants. But in the end he only spoils her so she takes everything he gives to her for granted.

A Pimp understands that a woman won't value what she's given for free or all the time, nobody does. By trying to earn her approval all of the time you ultimately put yourself in the position of submissiveness to her because you're pedestalizing her pussy over your energy like a trick.

A Pimp refuses to pedestalize sex over money and self growth. A Pimp gets it clear that sex is a mutually beneficial act for her and him, not just for his pleasure by never giving her sex only because she wants it. She has to earn sex from him.

That forces her to show him that she has more to offer than her body and it removes her feelings of entitlement due to her idea of pussy power. Now without her body as her bargaining chip she has to use her brain and her actions to impress you.

This puts the pressure on her to show she has more to a pimp than her body or seduction. She so used to using her body, her looks and her pussy to get whatever she wants out of men. Now she has a lot less confidence because she has a man in her life that makes her feel insecure.

A Pimp makes her pedestalize him and what he has to offer instead because he's highly educated and gamed up with wisdom and specific instructions for her to grow her life. He's the leader and he leads with his mouth.

Now she has to follow because she can't lead with her pussy. Every woman says that she wants a man that pedestalizes her, but she lusts for the man that she pedestalizes and she stays with a man that she pedestalizes.

She wants a man she looks up to and feels is more capable than her. She really desires to follow a masculine and powerful man she respects more than she loves. Deep inside, her feminine energy wants to follow a man so she can feel free from her cares and worries. She lusts for a man who allows her to be free.

Earning a man that she pedestalizes and looks up to because she feels safe and secure with him makes her feel like a little girl who won a prize that she can be proud of. This is why a man must learn that a woman's respect is much more important than her love.

A Pimp wants to have intellectual intercourse with her mind so he can take over her body. Because a woman's body will always follow her mind, not the other way around. He looks to mold his woman's mind, and not be controlled and molded by her mind.

If she molds you:

1. She'll lose her sexual attraction to you

2. You'll lose yourself

A Pimp instills his thinking in her, not the other way around. You can't allow her to program your thinking into hers, because she'll be the one in power. So a Pimp instills his thinking into her so he has the major control of her mind instead.

A Pimp only deals with women from a position of power. He understands the manipulation tricks that she uses to take power from weak men. Most men are always putting her in the major position of power over themselves because they're focused on getting pussy more than keeping the power.

Pimping Is An Art Form

To take on the mindset of a pimp you have to first learn the psychology behind how a woman thinks. You have to analyze and understand the general thought patterns, actions and habits of most women. This evens out the mental advantage that most women have over men.

Add your logic to your understanding of a woman's general thinking, and you'll always stay 2 steps ahead of her. Once you understand the psychology behind a woman's thoughts and actions you'll learn what a woman thinks before she thinks it.

Real Game Can't Be Seen

If people can see it, then it's not good game. That's because real game can't be easily spotted, that's what makes it so effective. So your game has to be smooth and without holes. This is why good game isn't filled with lies and deceit.

Good game is filled with the truth so she trusts it. Always remember that a woman will eventually find holes in your game if it's filled with lies because she's used to men in her past lying to her. Most women have trust issues because so many men are liars so she's waiting for you to lie to her so she can mistrust you.

So you have to always keep your game clean because all lies have an expiration date. Once she finds out that you're a liar she will never fully trust your game anymore. You want her to trust your game 100% of the time. And that level of trust is only established through you telling the truth consistently over time.

So to keep your game from being seen you have to always say what you do and do what you say to keep your words credible and trustworthy in her eyes. Most men think that having game means that you have to lie in order to effectively manipulate the thoughts and actions of others.

But to really have game means that you're using strategy like the game of chess to get people to move how you need them to move. So you have to understand human psychology and the primary motivations of the person you're dealing with so you can stay 2 steps ahead.

Because you can't move a person that you don't understand. This means that you have to learn, study and enhance your game always. If you want to be a master of the game then you can never stop learning. So be a sponge to knowledge and wisdom of all kinds.

And absorb thought provoking wisdom any chance that you can. This is the only way that you will upgrade your intelligence and level up your game. Never be lazy in learning because the more you learn the more power you possess.

The Game: The easiest way to understand the game is to always play it the opposite way that most men play it, that's how you win! Most men lie, so tell the truth. Most men are afraid to say what they feel, so always say what you feel, most men are focused on sex, so focus on her mind.

An intelligent man isn't looking just to raise her skirt, because the act of sex lasts only for a few moments. An intelligent man wants to raise her intelligence, because influencing her mind lasts a lifetime. And in return she will raise her skirt for you willingly.

That's Real Game!

The Pimp Game Is Everywhere

Everything in the world that uses the law of OPE = Other People's Energy to make money in this society is using the principles of pimping. The game just goes by a different name, but in the end it's all the same. The goal of pimping is always to make money.

Businesses pimp their employees by paying them just enough money to survive so they have to keep working for more. This type of pimping in the business world is no different than how a pimp controls the money of his ho's. He gives her just enough money to survive so she needs him.

A ho becomes a wage slave to her pimp just like an employee becomes a wage slave to the company they work for. The only difference between a ho and an employee is the product being sold. But ultimately regardless of the product being sold it's still the same pimping principles of capitalism.

In the concept of Capitalism one person or a group of people are capitalizing on the labor energy of others for their profit. In pimping and in business the goal is always still the same, MONEY! A pimp simply takes the product of pussy and female companionship to the marketplace and sells it to the world market.

While a company either creates a product or resells a product already made by others and sells it on the world market. There's 2 major motivations in the world sex and money. These 2 things motive every human being in the world.

For example, the natural desire for the pleasure of sex drives men and women to buy things they desire in hopes for sex. While money motivates people to work long hours for years upon years just to buy what they desire. A pimp understands the power of sex and the power of money.

You Have To Master Sexual Transmutation

This is the act of being able to transmute your sexual energy and desire for sex into an energy that can be used towards your goals and dreams. And once you replace your desire for sex with the desire for money, freedom, wealth and happiness, you'll become incredibly successful.

That's because the allure of sex is the most powerful stimuli known to humankind. Money and sex rule the world because there's nothing that we want more than money and sex. Men use money to buy sex and women use sex to get a man's money.

Your desire for sex can be transmuted which means to transfer into another desire that's more beneficial to your life. If you can take your desire for sex and turn it into a desire for money, you'll acquire anything and everything that you desire.

It's incredibly important for a pimp to master sexual transmutation because he's selling sex. If he gets high off his own supply then his ho's will take advantage of his weakness for sex just like she takes advantage of the trick.

A pimps high has to come from the desire for more money and not more sex. Because what makes the pimp a pimp in the first place is that he is thinks like a ho. So it's to his detriment if he thinks like a trick. Because his ho's will seduce him out of his money.

It's always money over pussy in the mind of a pimp. Even when it comes to giving his ho's dick, she only gets his sex as a reward for her doing what a pimp wants her to do. The pimp is powerful in the eyes of a ho because he plays the same game that she plays, he's just better at it than her.

Sex is a reward for a ho and not for the pimp because he sees money as his motivation. The pleasure of financial stability and being able to buy what you want is much more difficult to achieve than sexual pleasure because it comes with a much longer lasting high.

So turn your sexual appetite into a money appetite and you'll have more power over any woman that you deal with. If you can see past her body and focus on seducing her mind, her body will fall into your lap automatically. This is how a pimp plays the game.

All a woman has is her body to seduce you out of your money and your masculine energy. If she can seduce you enough to get what she wants out of you like your money or your relationship commitment then she captured your mind, instead of you getting hers.

Of course sex feels good but if you settle for the immediate gratification of sex over the long-term gratification of money, you will find yourself in the long run without both. So redirect this sexual craving into the craving for financial freedom and now you're thinking like a pimp.

Women want your money. And they give away access to their pussy everyday to men who'll pay to play. Because to a woman her pussy isn't important, but she does understand its importance to a man. That's why there'll always be a never ending line of tricks who will trade their money for her sex.

Your job as a pimp is to be different than the tricks who pedestalize pussy over money. Always put money over pussy and you'll have all the pussy you want as women chase you for money. That's playing the game like a pimp.

Either you can be like a trick and chase the cat, or you can have what the cat wants, so the cat will chase you. But your fist step is to transmute your desire for sex into the desire for money. Remember you're the ho and she's the trick! Let her trick for your dick!

Read People's Thoughts And Motives

If a pimp doesn't start learning from the beginning how to read body language and how to figure out what people are really saying, he's done before he starts. As a Pimp you must develop the ability to read new environments quickly with all of your senses and not just your eyes.

This game comes with plenty of smooth talking snakes and extremely beautiful women. If you get caught up thinking with your dick at the wrong time even once, that could be your life. You must have field awareness, like a quarterback in the pocket feeling the rushers pursuit around him.

If you can't feel what you don't see around you, then you'll lose your ho's to a pimp that can. The devil's in the details and in the things most people don't see or pay attention to. The details are where you as a pimp have to be paying the most attention whenever you're dealing with your ho's and other people.

To become a master pimp you must have the ability to understand body language like no other. People will say more with their eyes and their bodies than they do with their mouths. The mouth can say anything and it often does, but the body has a much harder time lying.

It's your job as a pimp to immerse yourself in the study of human psychology. If you can learn about basic human motivations and what body language cues show that people are lying then you'll read people like a book.

This game is mental and you have to always be reading your ho's, other pimps and the people in your environment so you can sense danger. Studying psychology will not only teach you how to read people better, you'll also understand how to disguise your body language when it's needed.

Pimp mastery is human psychology mastery. Most people don't study and learn to know thyself. Once you understand the motivations of yourself you'll understand the motivations of other people. Now you can use what you've learned to move people like you move a chess piece on a chess board.

Big Game Always Starts With Small Moves

Most guys want to be a giant in the pimp game immediately. But you have to pay your dues and make your mistakes like every other pimp because it's the only way you'll learn this game right. You have to master the details of the pimp game before real pimping comes alive in you.

Once you stop investing your time to learn in this game, you'll burn in this game. It's very important that you invest your free time in learning how to turn your ho money into long term and consistent streams of income.

This is where most pimps fail in the long run because they fall in love with the flash and blow their cash instead of building their stash. So learn how to invest into your interests and your ho's skill sets so you don't blow the dough.

The goal isn't to stay a pimp forever so don't fall in love with the fame or the fortune like most pimps do because it never lasts. If you can turn your game legit, even better. Take the paper you get from pimping and build companies that you can sell or build from the ground up.

Not only will it make you more money, your ho's will admire your ability to upgrade the quality of their lives so they'll stay dedicated to your game longer. But if you just take the dough and blow it, you better know that your ho's are watching how you handle the cash they sell their ass for.

And also if you don't upgrade your mind and the wisdom you have to entertain your ho's with, your game will get old and stale. Your ho's will get bored by your repetitive words and behaviors because you'll get predictable. Your predictability can mean the death of your game and maybe you.

If you let lazy and unproductive habits of thinking and behaving take root in your pimping eventually your hoes will detach from the hypnotism of your game. This will leave you with no hoes and no way to make more bread because ho's talk. Now your game will gain the reputation of being lame.

Make The "Big" Decisions

When she's relying on you for direction or you're confronted with a big decision, always have a solution and a solid point of view. If the issue's with one of your hoes and your point of view might blow the ho, let her go. One ho don't stop a show so go out and get you another one to replace her.

You have to make all the big decisions so they fall on you win or lose. Just like the superstar has to take the last shot, win or lose. That's why only having one ho is too close to having no ho's which is a no go! There's no other leader than you.

And any other ho competing for leadership will create a mutiny against you with the others. Eventually you'll say the wrong thing to her that ho, and it'll be the perfect words to push her totally against you into hate. There's a thin line between love and have.

Never make any decisions based on how many hoes you have and always make decisions by first looking at the biggest picture possible to figure out your best plans. Always weigh the costs and the benefits first before you make any decision.

And never make any decision based upon emotions alone. Whenever you make an emotional decision you've lost your pimping. All decisions have to be thought out and analyzed so you can make the right decisions that get you closer to the prize you seek.

See Through Problems To Find Solutions

Sometimes, shit can get extremely thick from the issues, worries and problems that your women have from time to time. A pimp has to see past all of the b.s. coming at him and spot the proper solution to the problem, while still finding a way to get paid at the same time.

A pimp isn't a problem revolver, he's a problem solver. So if you're the kind of person who gets panicked, stressed out and anxious when problems happen then pimping is not for you. Because this game is for the calm, relaxed and cool. This game is for the wise, not the fool.

If you can't be cool as ice in hot situations by staying calm during big issues then your hoes won't trust your leadership. And if your ho's don't trust your leadership skills then they'll find a pimp who can lead with calm and coolness during stressful situations.

Because contrary to the images you see on t.v and movies, the real job of a pimp isn't just riding around in fancy cars and clothes with ho's. A real pimp is a leader and guide for his ho's in the form of a counselor, teacher, mother, father and his ho's problem solver.

Your ability to show your ho's that they can depend on you to solve their problems will determine how effective you'll be as a pimp and how long you'll be in this game. If your ho's can't come to you to find solutions, they'll eventually find another pimp who will.

Invest In Your Overall Game Plan

You can't expect to be a successful pimp without investing in your future. Buying jewelry, clothes, the flyest cars, fabulous homes, penthouses and all of the toys you can imagine is a good start. But if a pimp wants to become the biggest, he has to use his money to become independent from ho money.

Make business man moves with your cash and don't fall into the trap of impressing other pimps in the game because it'll only get you killed. They won't admire you for what you have more than they'll hate you for having what they don't.

Have your moments of flash because it's part of attracting ho's into your stable, but make sure you first stack your cash. Keep what you have low because everyone's pocket watching in this game. And make more moves that people can't see, than the ones they can see.

Let the other pimps fall in love with paying cash for the flash that never lasts. Stack cash, invest cash, then buy the flash, in that order, ya dig! Remember your job isn't to stay a pimp forever because this game is brutal and extremely dangerous.

And put money away that your ho's don't know exist. Put money to the side that you can use as a backup plan just in case your pimping dies or your ho's leave. A smart pimp works his way out of this game by building something for himself that's independent from his ho's working for him.

This is how you play this game like a master. Your master plan has to be to leave the game and watch the other pimps struggle when they get older and their ho's leave, because they will. Most pimps don't make it out of this game rich. So be different and build something that you can be proud of.

Catching A Ho

"Treat her, like you meet her"

-Pimpin Ken

Be Ready To Catch A Ho At Any Time

A pimp never knows where the next ho's going to come from. She could be sitting at the bar waiting on a pimp to approach her, at the carwash, corner store, the supermarket or the movies. She truly can come from anywhere, so have your pimping sharp and always ready.

A pimp always has his game hot and ready for the next woman who wants to try her hand at this game. They'll come in all shapes and colors so don't be surprised by who approaches you. No woman should intimidate you because regardless of what she looks like they're all the same.

She wants to be pimped, but by the right pimp only. Once she meets you, you're like a scorpion lining its prey up for the strike. Line her up just right and strike with your pimp game at the right time. If you can read people, she'll show you exactly when it's the right time to strike.

So always dress the part when you leave the door and make sure that you present yourself like a man of class instead of trash. And never introduce yourself to a woman, present yourself to a woman as you're the prize because she's privileged to be in the presence of a real pimp.

Don't Get Stuck In A Conversation

You have to be able to shift your conversation quickly when you think this certain conversation is going to catch the ho. But you have to be able to switch up quickly if your game doesn't stick also. You must possess the kind of communication that massages both sides of her mind.

Add a little humor, with a little care and some manliness flirting to stimulate her attraction. A Pimp has the ability to see and feel quickly how her energy is responding to his words and actions. He then responds to her impulses with his pimpulses.

If she isn't catching your game, change it. As a pimp you must be able to change your flow of conversation at the drop of a dime. If you can't read her energy changes quickly, you'll miss her subtle cues. These cues are the clues that tell you what she's really thinking versus what she's saying.

Women like to speak with their bodies more than their words because they're afraid of emotional rejection. This is why it's so important as I stated before for you to study human psychology and non verbal communication.

As a pimp you have to read her body language and flow with the rhythm of her words. Stay calm and talk at the same pace she's talking. Let her talk and then pick the topics she speaks of that you want to expand on.

Then say some of the same words that she says because people subconsciously like when someone talks like them and uses the same pace they talk at. This strategy is called conversation manipulation. And this is how you keep the conversation going in the direction you want it to. A leader, leads her!

Always Pace Your Conversation

Sometimes a pimp's mind can be thinking so fast during a conversation that he doesn't realize he's left the ho's mind behind. Whenever you talk to a ho you need her mind to always be aligned with yours so she understands the game you're giving her.

You never want to confuse or lose the ho during a conversation ever! She has to be on the same page with you at all times. So talk at a slow and methodical pace and use purposeful pauses after you make important points that you want her to absorb.

Use eye contact when you speak and say what you mean and mean what you say with a calm but stern voice when you really need her to listen up. When you talk at a slow rate it forces people to listen harder and more intently.

It's the opposite of what most people think they have to do when they want to get their point across. Most people think if they yell more people will listen, but that does nothing but hurt people's ears. And people with hurt ears only want to get far away from the pain of that conversation.

They can't listening to what you have to say when they're trying to shut out the loud noises of your loud mouth. So be smooth, talk with a calm voice that shows others that you're in control of yourself and think out your questions and their answers thoroughly.

Anyone that talks a lot is insecure and lacks self awareness. Too much talking makes other people feel like you have something to prove due to your insecurity or feelings of inferiority. Don't be that guy! There's nothing for a pimp to ever prove to anyone, they need to prove themselves to a pimp.

So choose and use your words carefully. Because as a pimp your words are your most effective weapon in this game. Your words will either enhance your game or destroy your game.

Always Check A Ho's Background

Never be naive or stupid and just accept any new ho because she's pretty or down with your pimping. You don't know what a new ho has going on in her background because who knows where this ho came from.

She could be a junkie, running from another pimp, evading a past dangerous and abusive man among many other dangerous things. It's always good to do a quick background check and see what you can find out about her early on.

Don't trust a word she says and check if her words are valid. Check her past pimps, her work history, her online presence, her past boyfriends, her friends, criminal background, her family members and see if the ho has a sketchy past or not.

And if she gets caught up in one lie, cut the ho loose immediately. You can't afford a lying ho because that shows deception in the slightest form. If she's deceptive with her mouth, she sure in hell will be deceptive with her body.

Plus a lying ho is a major liability to your pimping. You can't afford to ever let anything sneak up on your pimping because ignorance isn't bliss. If you ignore things because she can get you a lot of bread, they'll eventually pop back up at the worst time in the future.

It'll be your fault for being absent minded and lazy because you didn't check the ho's background. You have to protect your pimping at all times. If you let just one thing slip by you it could mean the death of your game and even your death.

This game isn't a ball game for babies or lazy pimps only focused on the bread. You gotta always know where's the ho's head is by understanding her past so you can understand her future. A new ho with nowhere to go is a ho's whose background you better know!

Always Remember What You Say To A Ho

A Pimp must remember every promise that he makes to each of his ho's. You have to always remember what your stance is on a specific topic is and never change it for any ho. She can believe what she believes but what you believe can never change.

Never give a ho the confidence of feeling like she knows more than you by changing your opinion on something to match hers. Your opinion on whatever topic of discussion has to be solid and firm, regardless if she agrees with your not.

And never say anything out of your mouth to a ho that you don't intend on keeping. Integrity is big in this game. That means that you have to stand by what you say to a ho even if you don't feel like doing it after you said it.

So never say anything that will trap you in the future because once you say it to her you better do it. If you ever forget what you say she will lose respect for you and your word. A pimp has to keep her respect and if he loses it, he will lose that ho.

Your main job is to stand in the position as a leader and her God. God doesn't forget so you can't either. Don't make promises or say things that you don't mean and never get caught in lies. If you say it then do it, that's what a solid man does anyway. As a pimp you have to live and die by your words.

Don't Pimp Past One Ho, To Get A New Ho

This mainly applies when you're down on a fresh and new ho. A lot of new pimps see the pimping only as a fun game of getting women, but this game is very serious and very real. Too many pimps lose one ho trying to impress a new ho.

You can't be greedy with your ho's. Let your game set in on one ho first before you move to the next. This goes for every ho you get down for you. If you don't get her head locked into your game so she's down 100% with the whole plan, she will always turn on you when a new ho comes.

Ho's get jealous of other women very easily because women are naturally always in competition with each other. So make sure the first ho knows when you find a new ho and then keep her reassured of the bigger plan.

Reassure her that you recruiting this new ho is all a part of the bigger plan to get you both paid and not just for you to get laid. This reassurance from you will help her get past the initial jealousy she feels so she can regain focus on the bigger goal, instead of the new ho.

Even if she's a good ho who's been down with you she'll still get a little jealous. So the constant reassurance of her main position in your life is the key. Because she's still a woman who naturally wants all your attention to herself.

Once one is down and she knows her job without you having to tell her anymore, then start on the next recruits. Greed kills in the pimp game so don't ever forget that! Pay-tience and persistence is what pays the pimp the most money in the long run.

Choosing Vs Being Chosen

Whenever a woman chooses you, you've won already. That's because she's taken charge and shown her interest in you. And unlike the cold approach you're not diminishing your value by acting thirsty. Sometimes when you approach a woman she can perceive that as desperate.

When she chooses you, you don't have to worry about doing any of that. She's already taken away the pressure you would feel from initiating a conversation because she now has all of that pressure. Now you don't have worry about impressing her because she's taken the initiative to win your approval.

All that's left is the dating stage if you decide to choose her back. This gives you the power to speak to her with confidence. Because she's the person submitting to you because of her attraction to you. And when you've been chosen there's no need for a pickup line or the need to impress her.

She's taken charge to let you know she's into you. Because she did all of the initial work, you won't have to work to gain her attraction, you already have it. She already assumes that you'll know that she likes you, so now it's your choice to choose back or not.

Women expect you to know when she is choosing you. And when you know how to read her choosing signals it means that you have experience with women. Women don't have game, so her approaching you is all the game she has.

She'll use her words and her body language to make it clear to you that she's choosing you. She may look you into your eyes and touch your arm. So any time a woman touches you during conversation she is choosing you.

Choosing Signals

<u>The Soft Choose</u>: Soft choosing signals are the subtle gestures from a woman that shows she's interested in you. This can be a simple smile or a long glance of eye to eye contact with a shy turn away. Soft choosing signals are very subtle so most men miss these signs.

She soft chooses when something about you made her feel good. This can be the way you walk, the way you look or the way that her looking at you made her feel inside. Something about you makes her feel interested in you.

A woman chooses a man based upon how he makes her feel when she looks at him, even without direct contact. Most women will not just choose you only because she's attracted to you sexually. Her attraction is more often something she feels energetically about you that she likes.

While men choose a woman mostly based upon what she looks like and his sexual attraction to her. This is what makes men and women different when they choose a mate. Men choose based on looks, women choose based on energy.

Soft Choosing Signals:

• Long eye to eye contact
• A shy turnaround after eye contact
• Hair touching especially around the ear
• A blush is a major choosing signal

Never approach a woman based solely on a soft choosing signal. Only approach her if you're absolutely sure that she's ready for you to close the deal on. When you know that she's showing real choosing signals it'll give you more confidence when approaching her.

<u>The Hard Choose</u>: Converting the soft choose into the hard choose is where you give the woman a chance to show if she's really interested in you. Her soft choose will convert into a hard choose only after you talk to her.

If she shows only soft choosing signals, then she might not really be interested for whatever reason. She could just be smiling at you because she's nice. Or she could be interested in you but she already has a man at home she's committed to. Some women also just like male attention.

Hard Choosing Signals:

• Smiling at you excessively and looking at you
• Walking up to you and approaching
• Saying something flirty to you with obvious meaning
• Being all over you and touching you

If She Hard Chooses: Never let her to be the one to leave the conversation. You have to be the first one saying that you have to go, not her because it gives her the feelings of wanting to know more about you. If she leaves the conversation first you'll feel that way instead.

Ask her surface questions about herself, not personal or deep questions. Then don't let her lead the conversation. You should be the primary one asking questions about her so you can choose the topics to discuss further.

Keep the conversation surface because it keeps her intrigued into wanting to know more about you. You always want to be the one doing the most listening and asking the most questions. Because you'll keep your sense of mystery through avoiding talking about yourself.

<u>The Game</u>: Your job is simple, if she chooses close the deal!Put the pressure on her to talk and make her work for your energy. Don't make the mistake most men make of trying to earn her energy. Have the confidence that you deserve to be chosen.

Let her put in the most effort and then you reward her with your effort. This will make her feel blessed to have your presence because she has to earn your energy. You want to be the masculine energy in the conversation. And you do this more from listening than talking.

Always keep your composure by staying calm and talking in a slow pace. Don't talk too fast because you'll seem nervous, and over excited to be in her presence. Remember it's all about a methodical conversational dance. And if you act unconfident you'll blow it!

A Turnout Ho Vs A Burnout Ho

A <u>Burnout Ho</u> is a woman who has a lot of experience with men. She likely has a lot of kids and is only with a man for her own selfish needs like money, help parenting or a sexual partner. The only issue with a burnout ho is that her mind is set in its old ways of thinking.

She's a lot less likely to accept your game because of her trust issues and traumas from past relationships. And she carries a lot of emotional baggage from so many failed relationships, so she's lost hope in men altogether.

She has become disillusioned and burnt out on life and romantic relationships so her mind is closed to new and fresh game. A closed mind can't learn so you have to avoid closed minded women who are set in her ways because you can't teach them anything.

You don't even want to try and teach an old dog, new tricks because it will only cause you to get frustrated and angry. It's just easier and much less frustrating to just get a new dog. It's easier to teach someone what you've taught them, than to unteach what somebody else has already taught them.

A turnout ho must be able to empty her head of all of the old game from the past and trust your game completely with her mind and her efforts. She has to be ready to pay more than she weighs. This means that she has to be worth the effort of you teaching her new ways over her old ways.

A <u>Turnout Ho</u> is eager to learn because she hasn't had a lot of experience with different men. Her mind is fresh and open to new ideas because she still has hope for the future and she still possesses passion for the moment.

A turnout ho will always look to impress and please you, instead of only focusing on what pleases her because she's willing to listen to what a pimp needs. You need an open minded woman who is open to new suggestions.

You can always teach a new dog new tricks more than you can teach an old dog new tricks. Her mind has to be open for your game or else it's a waste of your time. You don't have the time to train an old ho who should already know. Just find a new ho that will listen!

Most Women Have Low Self Esteem

A woman's low self esteem is her weakness, so use it to your advantage! Most women have a low self esteem and as a pimp it's your job to find the area of low self esteem that's her weakness. Often it's her looks because of societies pressure for her to be perfect.

Her low self esteem makes her vulnerable to a pimp because once you find it you break her down because of it. Break her old mind down by making her feel ashamed of her lack of confidence and self esteem, then build her new mind up with confidence and flattery.

You have to break her down by destroying the old programming she has in her head so you can replace it with your words of confidence and self esteem. What you're doing is you're replacing the old thought patterns she has in her mind with yours so she feels better about herself.

You don't want low self esteem ho's because they're vulnerable to other men who flatter her and give her compliments just to manipulate her mind. You have to be the puppet master of her mind so she looks to you for validation of her self esteem instead of other men.

If you're the man responsible for building her self esteem up it'll make her look at you as her hero. And because you tore her old ways of thinking about herself down, and then you built her back up to become better than she was before, she'll feel like she owes you for her growth and change.

Her weak mind and low self esteem makes it easier for you to reprogram her. A weak mind is the best trait to find in a person that you want to re-program because it's vulnerable due to its lack of direction. You can't tear down a woman with a strong self esteem easily.

That's because a strong minded woman isn't going to do anything for you that she doesn't first want to do. A woman with a high self esteem has a high regard for herself and that makes it very difficult to reprogram her mind.

There's No Loyalty In This Game

Loyalty is very, very rare so never put all of your trust in one ho because you never know what tomorrow will bring. Always remember that a woman is likely to go to another pimp eventually regardless of how strong your game is. That's because curiosity always kills the cat!

Other ho's bragging about their pimp and her curiosity of other men in the game will pull her towards disloyalty at all times. And one day she will let her mind and her imagination about another pimp get the best of her. Don't be fooled by her vows of loyalty to your pimping, it's game!

Because a ho can blow at any moment, never tell her all of your personal business. Because when she leaves your pimping, your personal business, your secrets and your reputation is always going to leave right along with her.

And one thing that you can surely count on with a ho is that she'll talk about your business to the next pimp and his ho's. She'll tell them all the good, the bad and the ugly of your life if you tell her too much because you trusted her too much.

Let a ho tell you all of her business, instead of you telling her all of your business. And then make sure that you keep any of your problems, worries, weakness and your game plan to yourself regardless of how down the ho has been. Every ho is capable of deception just like a square woman.

Then always stay a stand up man. It's your job to make sure that you don't do things that you'd be ashamed of her telling others. And don't abuse the ho mentally or physically because she'll be happy to spread your business to the streets out of spite to ruin your reputation with prospective ho's.

So always stay prepared for her betrayal in this game just in case. Trust is truly a commodity that you can't afford because it's more expensive than you can imagine. Not even money can keep a ho down with you once her mind starts looking outside of your pimping.

Women Trust Honesty

Earn a ho's with trust with honesty, not deception and dishonesty. Lies and deceit are not good game because you'll lose a ho's respect and her trust every time. If you lie to her, she will lie to you and if you deceive her, she will deceive you. That's the rules in the game of pimping and the game of life!

Women feel that if you're honest with her, she can trust you to continue being honest. It makes a woman feel comfortable if she can trust your words. And she'll listen to what you say much quicker than if she has to always question them.

This means that you have to always be honest and straight up in every situation with a ho, even if you know it'll hurt her feelings. Because she'll trust you even more if you're brutally honest and say what you feel and not what you want her to hear.

This is why square men are always losing with women. They tell her what she wants to hear instead of what she needs to hear so they never trust their honesty. You're not a scary square, you're a powerful pimp, that's what separates you from them.

Women appreciate the hard truth even if she gets upset at it initially. After the truth you gave to her sinks in, she'll know you're not just some scary square who's afraid to lose her because you'll tell her the truth even if it makes her angry. And she'll respect that you're a real man that doesn't lie.

She'll Add Or Be Bad For Your Pimping

For a ho to be a benefit to you, she must add and not subtract from your life. If she doesn't come in willing to give freely, let her get gone quickly back to the streets. A subtracting ho only came to take what you have. There's nothing that you can do with a selfish woman of any kind but get burnt.

She will only take your energy, your money and waste your valuable time because she's not looking out for anyone but herself. Subtractors aren't just gold diggers, or seducers like most men think. You can never compromise your growth for any woman especially a selfish and self centered ho.

If she wants you to stop building your dreams and put them on hold for her dreams or she holds you back in any way, then she has shown herself as a subtracting woman. So she'll only ruin the progress that you're building in this game.

There is no compromise of your goals and dreams that you can make when a woman wants to be down with your game. It is her job to compromise her goals and her dreams for the bigger picture of your dreams period. If she can't add to your pockets then she gotta get gone fast as a rocket!

Your Happiness Gotta Be Her Happiness

Your presence is a gift in a woman's life because you're a man with a plan. You have a solid dream with action steps that you're taking to make it happen, she does not. So if she's not willing to do what you need her to do, then you don't need her in your presence.

Another woman will fill that position in your life better than her if she thinks that her lack of plan is better than your plan. Any ho you pick in this game must admire your life and want to trade her old life for yours. She has to desire the life that you live now, and the life you will in the future.

But it's only through her loyalty to you and her obedience can she prove that she's worthy of the dream that you're going to achieve with or without her. This means that she has to dedicate her life to helping you achieve your dream life so she can benefit also.

Your happiness must equal her happiness and not the other way around. So you have to teach her that a pleased man, pleases his woman. And a pleased man doesn't have the desire to abandon a woman that dedicates her life to making her man happy.

When a woman is truly dedicated to you with her heart and only desires to see you happy, a man feels a deeper attraction and dedication to her. This means that she has to commit to your goals and dreams for your happiness first.

A ho that doesn't put the happiness of a pimp first gotta go. If she's only focused on making herself happy then she'll do selfish things that'll sabotage your progress just for her own benefit. Selfishness is what creates a manipulative and deceptive ho. And a deceptive ho will set you up!

The Pimping

"It's not about a pimp breaking a ho, it's about the woman breaking herself and bowing down to the privilege of your pimping."

-Pimpin Ken

The 8 Levels Of Pimping

Level #1: The game to get a woman to give you what you want and what you ask her from her without her fighting back. This is the basic relationship level of a pimping partnership and the basic level of all relationships.

Everyday couples have achieved this level of understanding. This is what a woman does when she's in love with you. It's easy to establish this level of the game with a woman who likes you enough to be in a relationship with you.

Level #2: The game to get a woman to do things for you that she never thought that she would do for anyone. This is called imprinting a woman because you will be permanently in her mind as the first man to ever get her to do this for you.

You have set a new standard in her life and that makes her associate forever this act with you. This is like taking a girl's virginity so she'll never forget you. You will always be the first one to get her to do it and she'll always be tied to you emotionally because you were the first.

Level #3: The game to get a woman to give you everything that she's worked for. For her to give you all the money she has and to give you what she put in the hard work to earn just because she loves you and wants to be with you.

She wants to earn you and pay her way just to have your presence around. She will part with everything that you want her to part with and give it to you just to be with your pimping. This means that she will even compromise her morals and values for you if it means your happiness.

Level #4: The game is to get a woman to do anything under the sun that she can think of for you, just to make you happy. That means that she will sacrifice her own happiness, her self worth and her self esteem for you just because she has to have you in her life so badly.

She fears to lose you so much she'll do nearly anything for you if she thinks that it's what you need or what you want her to do to satisfy your wants and needs. She'll break the law if you want her to and maybe even kill for you if you need it.

Level #5: The game to get a woman to accept that you have another woman in your life and she has to be down with it. She'll get past her own jealousy just because she wants you in her life so badly and she just can't lose you in her life.

She'll get over her own female nature which is to be possessive of her man and jealous of other women just to have your presence around. For her to give you everything she has and to still know that you have another woman means that she feels like she needs you in her life.

Level #6: The game to get the woman to not only know that you deal with another woman, but to live in the same house with her and be at peace. Not just knowing you have another woman but to become friends with the other woman and help her in any way that she can.

To make sure that the other woman has what she needs and to be fine with them both sharing a man in the same house. To know that tonight you won't be sleeping with her, you'll be sleeping with the other woman and giving her all of your attention tonight.

Level #7: The game to get her to understand that not only are you going to live with another woman in the same house, but if you want her to bring you another woman she will. To understand that she benefits when you add more women to the team to achieve the dream.

Level #8: The game to get her to understand that if you're with a woman sexually and you can't fully satisfy her, she's going to help you do that. If you need her to fulfill one of the woman's sexual desires tonight, not only is she willing to help you do that, she'll satisfy her for you if it's necessary.

She'll have sex with another woman for you because that's what you want her to do. She will go beyond her boundaries and preferences because the name of the game for her is she'll do anything to make you happy. Pimping is an art and you have to take it level by level to master this game!

The 3 Stages Of Breaking A Ho

Stage #1: The Recruitment - Enticing a girl through any means to get her attention for enough time to get her emotionally bonded to a pimp.

Stage #2: The Grooming - Using material goods, selling her a dream of their "perfect" life together, then learning her desires and weakness as a form of mind control and manipulation.

Stage #3: The Turnout - The use of love and fear by breaking a ho down and then building her back up to really build her self esteem for a pimps purpose. And then showing her love by giving her gifts and words of affection.

Repeating indoctrination of isolation mental programming phrases like "Nobody will love you like I do or treat you like I do because they don't understand you like I do." Your job as a pimp is to make her see you as God, so she'll follow you wherever you go like a lost puppy.

How To Capture Her Mind

Step #1: Do everything that you can do to be the best boyfriend that she's ever had! Go out of your way to make sure that she sees you as the man of her dreams.

Step #2: You do this by getting her very comfortable with you by letting her talk about herself and her life. So be a very good listener and take note of what she's saying.

Step #3: Then get her to talk deeper about her problems, traumatizing experiences and her dreams. Listen very closely to her trauma points.

Step #4: Make her believe that you have also gone through the same negative things that she did, but in your own way like you both share the same pain.

Step #5: Once you listen to her problems and her dreams, get her into thinking that you understand what she's been through and you will end her problems and make her dreams come true if she commits her life to your vision.

The information that she gives you will become her weakness that you'll exploit her with. You get her to talk about herself so that you could find her weaknesses and her vulnerabilities.

Step #6: Go out of your way to get close to her mentally and emotionally by making her feel like nobody understands her like you do.

The more she has turmoil in her home and dysfunction in her family life, the easier it is for you to manipulate this weakness to get her to move with you so she's under your control.

Step #7: Take her out and wine and dine her to give her a feel of "the good life" that she'll have with you as her man

Step #8: Stay persistent in how you pursue her by calling her everyday in a caring way and having her side in everything to solidify your influence in her daily thought life.

Step #9: Once she gets hooked into you emotionally, then turn into the distant one at the peak of her emotional bonding. This will make her feel like she needs you in her life to feel emotionally secure (The all in, all out trick)

Step #10: Repeat to her in different ways and words like "Nobody in the world cares for her the way that you do and nobody will understand her like you do". "Do "_____" for me because nobody is going to love you like I do."

Or "I'm your only true friend, your other friends are just using you or they just want to be you and have what you have because you're with me."

Step #11: Then distance her from her negative friends and family by demonizing them so that you have full control over her mind. Make sure that you express to her that they're the bad guys in her eyes.

Once she's emotionally involved and in love with you then use her feelings against her to say things like a woman that loves me would do "_____" for me to show it."

Step #12: Then reward what she does for you with gifts and appreciation to keep her incentivized to keep doing what you want her to do.

Make promises to her of future gifts and rewards if she keeps doing the simple things that you ask her to do for you. Giving her rewards along the way helps to make your promises more believable. Sell her the dream!

Be Cold When You Need To Be

As a pimp you must have the ability to turn your attitude cold when it's necessary. This is not a suggestion, this is a necessity for your survival in this game. Being cold serves two very important purposes in this game of pimping.

1. When you have to be unreadable by others to disguise your game. Emotions in this game is dangerous because the streets force pimps and ho's to read body language for survival. If your body language shows your hand just like poker you're done and so are your ho's.

2. The second purpose is when you have to get cold on a ho. If she can tear up and melt your heart you're not cut out for pimping. If you can't show her an occasional glimpse of your coldness, she'll eventually test you to see if she can take advantage of you.

The secret to being cold is saying how you feel and not fearing the consequence even if you do fear the consequences. If you face a ho head on most of the time she'll submit because she was just testing you to see if you have balls or not.

Keep Her Dependent On You

Control her ability to get what she needs by staying in charge of the money she earns. Because the more dependent she is on you, the more power you have over her survival needs and the harder it will be for her to leave you.

The government uses this strategy to control the people. They just control the cost of living and the wages by making sure the wages are slightly below the cost of living. That's why jobs pay you just enough money to live on so that you can barely stay ahead to survive.

Now you have to go back to work because your bills, survival needs and your wants are more than what you earn monthly. The government also uses credit to keep you in debt so you can buy more than you can afford which increases your dependance on the system.

Use the same strategy that the government uses with a ho by keeping her feeling in debt to you. Keep her in debt financially and also keep her in debt of what she owes to you for helping change her life for the better. Do this by making her believe that her life is so good because you're in it.

Show her your positive impact in her life and how she's a better woman because you're in it. And convince her that she wouldn't do well in life without you. Because in most cases she wouldn't do better than she is now without access to your game.

How To Maintain And Work Multiple Ho's

It's a learned art to pimping multiple ho's at the same time, especially more than three. Most pimps don't know how to pimp multiple women without choosing a main one as his favorite. Never designate a main ho as your favorite because it creates division between them.

Even the bottom bitch has to know her position and that she'll get put out and replaced if she acts out of a ho's place. If you let your ho's choose your pimping, there is no way you should be forced to choose one of them over the others.

They won't like the one that you chose as the main ho out of their jealousy. And because ho's are catty they'll gang up on her out of their jealousy. Keep your game objective and let each ho know her position personally, but be very careful what you tell a ho about another ho.

Don't divide your ho's with gossip or by allowing them to gossip about each other. They must see each other like sisters so they can work together. And always expect a ho to tell the others what you say because she can't help but say what's on her mind. All women talk too much!

If you show favoritism to a ho she'll use her position as a weapon against the other ho's, especially if they attack her or make her angry. So never tell one ho she's your favorite. They're all your favorite because they chose the right pimping period!

There's No Friends In The Game

When pimping begins, friendship ends! So you can never completely trust anyone in this game. Friends are dangerous because they'll always try to compete with you to have more than you. That's because no man wants to be second place and every man wants to be the King!

Friends are always pocket watching to compare if you have more than them. And they'll always gossip to other people outside the friendship you may not know about what you have. This makes you vulnerable to outside enemies so be cautious about what you show and tell your friends.

Expect some friends to hate. Whenever you align yourself with a man who feels less than you or has less than you, you'll lower his self esteem when he's around you. That's because he'll see you as a superior man and himself as an inferior man because you have more than him.

Some friends want to live your life first hand so they might try to sneak their way into your position. So they'll steal your stuff, ask to drive your cars, wear your clothes or try and sleep with your woman just to feel like you for a moment.

That's because jealous friend thinks that the only way that he can feel like "somebody" is by undermining you and making you feel less than him. So protect yourself at all times from jealous friends and expect disloyalty from other men.

A Pimps Word Is His Sword

Communication is always the best policy and always the best choice in this game. We're in this game to get paid so there isn't any sense in a pimp killing another pimp over some ho shit. We're pimps and damn sure not boxers who want to go to prison over an ego and miss out on the money.

We have plenty of conversation for occasions like that, that's what makes us pimps. But, if it's absolutely necessary a pimp will get busy and you have to know when that time is. Handle all of your problems with conversation without physical confrontation in most situations.

But always keep your surroundings in check. If you have to go to a dangerous environment keep a weapon or two handy. A knife is your best friend just in case. But your mouthpiece should always be your most effective weapon in the game.

Your tongue has to be mightier than the sword. Because your mouth can get your ass out of situations that not even a weapon can get you out of. So keep your mouthpiece sharp and ready for any situation. That's your job as a pimp!

The Trick Always Gets "Tricked"

A pimps always puts money over women, while a trick puts women over everything. That's why he'll pay his way just to be around women. Trick are the major clients of a pimp, strip clubs and porn sites. Businesses preying on a trick money creates billion dollar industries that are run by pimps.

The trick is called a trick because he's too lazy to put the work into her mind himself. He just decides to shortcut the whole process and pay the game with his hard earned money for her pussy. But he never gets the woman or her respect in the process.

The trick always gets tricked by the ho in the end because he'll never get his money's worth from just getting the pussy, because a ho's pussy is God given and she'll never run out of it. But making money takes time from his life for him to earn. So exchanges what's free to her for what he works for.

Ultimately the trick loses his self respect and the pimp keeps her self respect. And because the pimp doesn't elevate the woman over himself he can look in the mirror with confidence that he hasn't compromised his value to a woman just for pussy.

It's Macaroni, And Not Matrimony

There's no successful pimp who is married to one woman. Because once you get married to her, she know has leverage over you. She can get half of your things by getting you to sign a government marriage contract that benefits you in zero ways.

Marriage kills your masculine energy because a woman will look to gain access to the inner secrets and workings of your life and use them to get you to submit to her rules. And it'll be death to your game if you let any woman get close enough into your inner life to know your secrets.

A married man has to submit to her control because she now has the government backing her once you sign legally binding marriage documents. So she knows that if she leaves you that she will not leave with nothing.

This will make you naturally submissive to her because she now has more of an ability to ruin your life. And when you become more submissive to her, you'll feel like less of a man and lose your masculine energy over the course of the marriage.

Your masculine power comes from your independence from a woman's draining energy and not your dependance on her. You want her chasing you as the catch because once she catches you, the thrill for her is gone.

Her whole goal as a woman is to change you into the "perfect" man that she thinks she wants. But once she starts changing you into what she wants you to be, you'll lose your independence, your masculine energy and your pimp game.

Only a submissive man gets forced to check in with his woman every couple of hours and comes back exactly at the time that she says she wants him to, even when he isn't ready to leave. No pimp can be controlled by a woman if he wants to keep her respect. So marriage is a big no-no in this game!

Your Feelings Will Cost You

If you catch feelings, your pimp game is done! That's because feelings fog your vision and your decision making skills will get blinded by your emotions. As a man you're built to run off of logic and not on emotions.

Pimping is about business and not about love. You cannot bring love into your game and into your business. Because in business you can't commit to love, it'll only get you manipulated and resentful from being taken advantage of.

Always stay focused on the goal of money before pussy. You have to commit yourself, your mind and your actions fully to the bottom line like a fortune 500 company. The goal is the only focus, not falling in love. She can fall in love but not you.

Stay focused on the facts by using your knowledge of female manipulation and logic, not your feelings for the woman and your emotions. A ho will often try to get you in your feelings to throw you off your game and to manipulate your decision making but always stay cool.

Keep your decisions fact based by focusing on the bigger picture and by weighing the pros and cons of every decision you make. If you let feelings both positive and negative drive your decisions, or react emotionally you'll lose your game and your ho's.

Give A Ho Motivation And Inspiration

It's your job to keep a ho motivated. So always make sure that she has a reward for her work to keep her focused and feeling like what she's doing is actually paying off. Because if you don't keep her motivated with future goals to accomplish and material rewards she'll get discouraged quickly.

We all need an incentive to reignite our motivation when it loses steam. So reward her good behavior, her loyalty and her obedience with the things that she desires. If you always inspire her with incentives she'll work hard for you and for the rewards she gets from her effort.

All successful people have an internal and external incentive that inspires them to become greater. So the more she accomplishes, the greater you reward her. A woman is always asking herself "Is this relationship worth it?"

But if she's getting something out of being with you, the less likely she'll leave because she doesn't want to lose the rewards she's getting. So never let her feel like she's getting nothing out of the relationship because she will certainly leave. This goes for a ho or any woman you deal with.

Because a woman with no incentive to work hard in the relationship for a reward will fall behind and get discouraged over time. Nobody wants to work for nothing. And regardless of how good your sex is, or how tight your game is, it won't be enough by itself to keep her.

No rewards, you"ll have no woman, it's that simple in this game. The Business world works exactly the same way. Businesses and big companies dangle bonuses, raises, promotions over a workers head to give them an incentive to work hard.

Employers know that if there's no incentive to inspire hustle in people, the workers will only give the job just enough effort to not get fired. This is why women get comfortable, tired and lazy on their men. Without a reward there's no incentive for her to stay sexy for you or respectful of you.

Most men think that they can just buy flowers or take her to dinner on occasion, but it's not enough and it's not strategic. Listen to your women and reward them with what they love after they put in work, not before. Never reward her for just being your woman because you'll just create a spoiled woman with expectations.

Reward her for her productivity, for doing what you ask, and for her obedience. Because if she can be lazy and still get flowers, vacations and dinners, she'll stay comfortable and get fat, lazy on you. She needs an incentive in the form of a reward to work in the relationship and as a ho. Remember no reward, no ho!

Always Stand On What You Say

Always stand on what you say because your word is your bond in this game! You have to always be able to stand on what you say and never be afraid to say how you feel to a ho or anyone else ever. If you can't stand on your word, then you have no game to stand on.

You can't lead anyone with words that don't align with your actions, that's a hypocrite. Speak your truth and live it at the same time with no apologies. In this way you'll set yourself apart from all of the fakes in the game who use lying and fakery as their only game.

When they inevitably fall and become seen as the fake, you'll stand strong as the real because your word was your bond and your game was solid. Time will always reveal the truth just like time will also reveal a lie. If you get caught even once in a lie, then you're now looked at forever as a liar.

So don't mince your words or hesitate to say what you want to say to anyone. Of course you have to choose your words and how you say it wisely but that just being strategic and knowing your audience. If you're talking to another pimp then be respectful, and even when you're talking to your ho be respectful.

Make sure you're using eye contact effectively also. You're not a gangster, you're a pimp so you have to give respect to get respect in this game. As long as you say what you need to say calmly with strong eye contact, the person you're talking to has to take your words or leave them.

Never Allow Her To Disrespect You

Never allow disrespect in any way shape or form from anyone. Allowing disrespect in any way is a sign of weakness that's seen immediately by whoever disrespects you. Never allow a ho, another pimp, a trick, not even your momma to get away with any disrespect of you.

Allowing disrespect towards you in any way shows that the person you're dealing with doesn't fear your words or fear the retribution of your actions. Fear is a necessary element in this game because it'll make people second guess trying you if they fear you.

If they don't fear you in this game they'll steal your ho's, your ho's will leave and you'll lose your masculine energy. Masculine energy is what makes you a pimp! So always keep your masculine energy intact and protect it by any means by standing up immediately at any sign of disrespect from anyone.

As soon as the disrespect happens, address it immediately but calmly and don't wait until later. Never react emotionally or without thought, be strategic. When it comes to your ho's don't reprimand her from a place of anger, reprimand her from a place of principle.

Deal with the facts of the situation and not the feelings of the situation. You do this by telling her what she did wrong and why it can never happen again. If she wants to argue and fight then you tell her to find her way out the door. You don't ever fight with a ho, just tell her ass to go!

There's always another ho where she came from so don't ever look like you're stressing over her leaving even if you are. She can't see your weakness over her ever! And if she sees one ounce of weakness in you, she's got you.

If there's other people around or you're at a classy place pull her away from the group. Tell her with a calm voice and strong eye contact that "this kind of behavior will not be tolerated" by you again without you leaving.

This is a no compromise situation because you can never tolerate her disrespect. Be willing to walk away from the relationship if she disrespects you and show no remorse for it. This is a time to be cold in what you say and how you behave. One less ho, won't stop the show! The show always goes on!

Never Let Tears Melt Your Pimping

Women are the best actresses in the world. So if she can play you mentally and emotionally with her tears then the next step is she'll choose another pimp. If you can't see through her tears and female manipulation, you're going to get pimped by your ho.

Emotions are the worst thing to show and have in this game. There's so many negative things that a pimp sees in pimping that if you're too soft hearted or weak-minded you'll drink and drug yourself to death because of the trauma you get from pimping.

This is why so many of the former pimps in this game are broke, alcoholics, drug abusers, mentally scarred and homeless. This game isn't for the weak minded, scared, soft, weak hearted or easily manipulated person because it's not an easy game.

You have to put your kindness and empathy to the side so you can be cold as ice and use your mind over your emotions when you need to be, which is often. So over time you can lose touch with your emotional self and become cold hearted.

So whenever a ho starts crying make her leave until she can talk with her brain, and not with her feelings. Don't allow her to talk to you until she can talk to you without emotions. This forces her to deal with the facts instead of her feelings.

Once she sees that she can't manipulate you with her tears, she'll stop trying to. But this is going to take a while so be consistent because women are emotional by nature. She's used to getting her way by shedding a couple of tears. Just stay strong in your pimping and she'll learn tears don't work!

Gorilla Pimping Ain't Good Pimping

A gorilla pimp is different from a finesse pimp because he uses his fists instead of his words. He uses fear instead of an illusion love to make a woman submit to his game. He doesn't have the patience to play the game so he uses fear to get his way with her.

There are two ways to get anyone to follow your lead and they are either with fear or love. When you use love to lead a woman you can create trust, loyalty and dedication to your game without always fearing her deception.

But when you use fear to lead a woman you can count on her deception and disloyalty behind your back. That's because she's only listening to you out of her fear of pain. Once you're gone and you can't hurt her, she'll jump ship on you immediately.

You can't make money consistently in this game if your ho's keep leaving you because they're scared. This game is all about finesse because a hurt ho gets you no money. A hurt ho can get you put in jail when she feels like it'll help her get away from your fists of fury.

Hurting a ho can even get you killed by her brothers or other men she befriends. Being a gorilla pimp just shows that the pimp has emotional baggage and lacks the emotional maturity to use his words instead of his fists.

A gorilla pimp will never become a master pimp in this game because he's too emotionally unstable and emotionally immature. His focus is too much on the money instead of making sure that the honey is feeling safe and secure in his pimping.

This makes his mindset like a woman's because he's constantly making emotional mistakes that he regrets later. His anger makes him easy to manipulate by his ho's and by other pimps looking to take his ho's because he's weak minded.

All a pimp has to do is just wait for him to get angry and hurt one of his ho's and she'll look to find a less aggressive pimp. Just like any man who abuses his girl thinking that he's creating her obedience with is physical and or verbal abuse.

Physically abusing her only creates the desire for rebellion and disloyalty in his women. She'll leave him as soon as a smooth talking and less aggressive man speaks to her, because she's already looking for a way out. Ruling through fear and pimping with your fists always backfires on a pimp in the end.

There's only 5 endings for a gorilla pimp:

1. He kills her from his abuse by hitting her one too many times

2. He goes to jail for putting his hands on his ho's, another pimp or someone else

3. Death due to an angry father figure, another pimp or the brother of one of his ho's

4. Death due to the hands of his ho that he's hit one too many times

5. One of his ho's tell the police by snitching on him that he's pimping

As you can see the ending for a gorilla pimp is only death or prison. The only thing that differs is the way that he'll fall. But he will always fall to a bad ending in this game of pimping because violence will always meet more violence.

This game of pimping is all about possessing the mind of a woman and not just her body. If you only possess power over her body from using your fists, her mind will eventually take her body away from you as soon as she gets the chance.

You have to penetrate her mind and her body with your words and not your fists. If you can possess her mind with your words, then her body will follow automatically. Real pimping is all about owning a ho's brain. That's the real Game!

THANK YOU FOR READING

If You Received Useful Tools In This Information, Please Give Me A 4-5 Star Rating!

This serves as a reward for an author. It takes hours and months, sometimes years of no pay to put together books for the purpose of sharing information you see as important to the world.

Please just take out a minute of your time and please leave a quick positive review. Thank you tremendously for taking out the time to read this information and knowledge.
If you really took this information seriously and you applied the key principles into your daily life, I KNOW you are seeing results.

So again, I thank you for your interest in learning and any investment in applied knowledge will always be a winning investment.

NOTES